LONDON
ABC

The Random House Group Limited supports the Forest Stewardship Council (FSC®), the leading international forest certification organization. Our books carrying the FSC label are printed on FSC®-certified paper. FSC is the only forest certification scheme endorsed by the leading environmental organizations, including Greenpeace. Our paper procurement policy can be found at www.randomhouse.co.uk/environment.

LONDON

A   B   C

A   DOUBLEDAY   BOOK

978   0   857   53170   4

Published in Great Britain by Doubleday, an imprint of Random House Children's Books A Random House Group Company This edition published 2012

1 3 5 7 9 10 8 6 4 2

RANDOM   HOUSE   CHILDREN'S   BOOKS
61-63   Uxbridge   Road,   London   W5   5SA

w w w . k i d s a t r a n d o m h o u s e . c o . u k
w w w . r a n d o m h o u s e . c o . u k

Addresses for companies within The Random House Group Limited can be found at: www.randomhouse.co.uk/offices.htm

THE RANDOM HOUSE GROUP Limited Reg. No. 954009

A CIP catalogue record for this book is available from the British Library.

Printed and bound in China

LONDON
ABC

ILLUSTRATED BY

BEN HAWKES

DOUBLEDAY

WELCOME TO LONDON!

London is one of the most famous and iconic capital cities in the world. It is busy, bustling and full of treasures for you to discover. It's a centre for fashion, films and food, business, the arts and entertainment. Plus it's filled with countless museums, galleries, theatres, sporting grounds, shops, markets, parks and palaces. We are excited to show you some of these in this ABC!

Most of all London is full of stories – its history stretches back over 2,000 years, and it has been immortalised in hundreds of books, TV series and movies: from Dickens's Victorian London, to the London of Sherlock Holmes, Mary Poppins and Doctor Who.

We can't wait for YOU to explore London and start your own story. There are so many ways to discover the city: on foot, finding hidden side streets; on the underground (do you know which colour is for which line?); on red London buses or in black cabs. Remember to take care crossing the road and always have an adult with you!

And don't forget to take this little book with you too. On each page there are lots of things for you to spot beginning with that letter. Some are London things and some aren't! See if you can spot them all, and then turn to the back of the book to check your answers. We've also suggested some other London landmarks for you to seek out. And see if you can spot what our lost little penguin friend is up to as well.

Have fun exploring the London in this book, and the real-life one outside your door . . .

A IS FOR AQUARIUM

B IS FOR

BIG BEN

C IS FOR

E IS FOR EYE

F IS FOR FISH & CHIPS

G IS FOR

GLOBE

H IS FOR

HYDE PARK

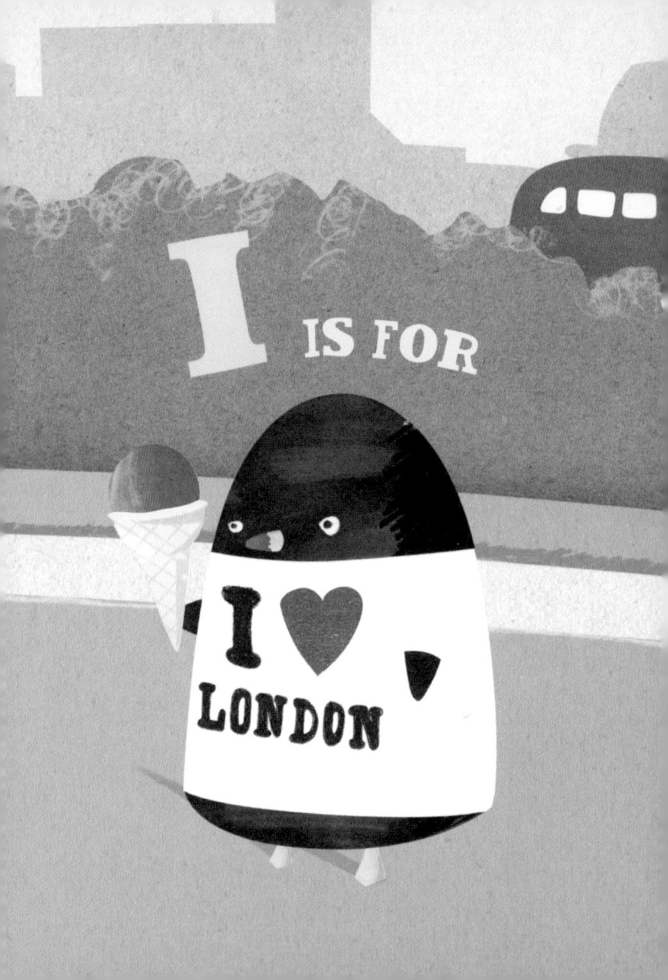
I IS FOR
I ♥
LONDON

chocolate VANILLA STRAWBERRY

J IS FOR

K IS FOR KEW

L IS FOR LORD MAYOR'S SHOW

M IS FOR **MARATHON**

MAP OF LONDON

N IS FOR

NELSON'S COLUMN

O IS FOR **OXFORD CIRCUS**

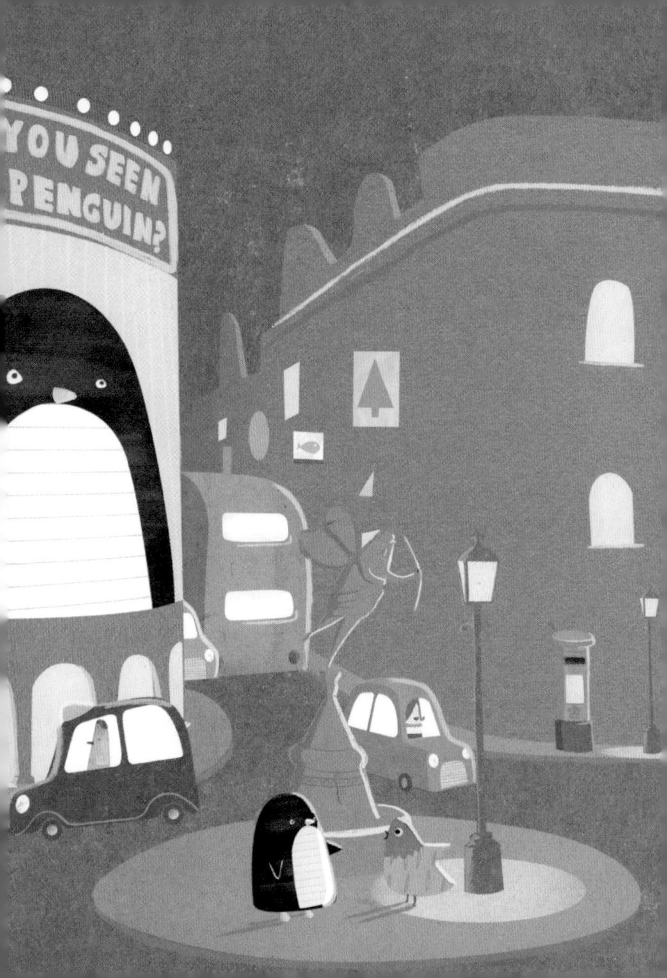
YOU SEEN
PENGUIN?

Q IS FOR QUEEN

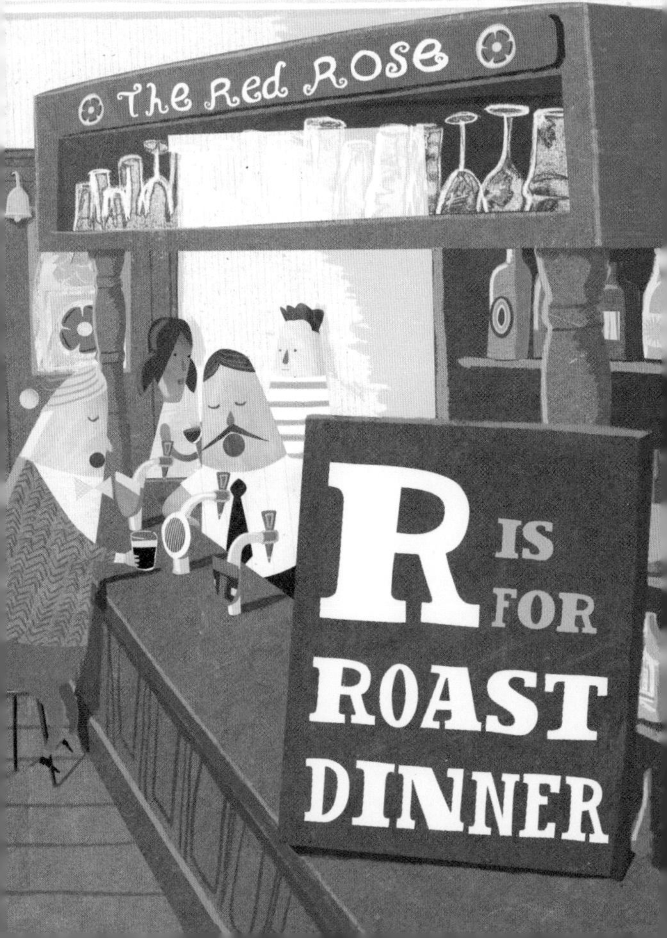
The Red Rose
R IS FOR
ROAST
DINNER

S IS FOR

STADIUM

T IS **FOR**

TOWER BRIDGE

U IS FOR

UNDERGROUND

LEICESTER
SQUARE WC2
CITY OF WESTMINSTER

V IS
FOR

W IS FOR WIMBLEDON

Y IS FOR

YOGA

Z IS FOR **Zoo!**

DID YOU SPOT?

A IS ALSO FOR: Anchor, apple, aquanaut

B IS ALSO FOR: Bearskin, bicycle, black cab, boat, bobby, bridge, Buckingham Palace, bus

C IS ALSO FOR: Camera, case, cat burglar, crown, cushion

D IS ALSO FOR: Dog, door, doorknob

E IS ALSO FOR: Elephant, English flag (St George)

F IS ALSO FOR: Fedora, fire bucket, fire engine, fire hose, firemen, fish, football

G IS ALSO FOR: Gallery, gentleman, Gherkin, glasses

H IS ALSO FOR: Hair, hat, hedge, helicopter, helmet, horse, hot dog, hugs

I IS ALSO FOR: Ice cream, ice-cream van, insect, iris, iron gates

J IS ALSO FOR: Jelly, jug, juggler, juggling balls

K IS ALSO FOR: Kate, King (to be), kiss, kite, kitten, knitter

L IS ALSO FOR: Ladder, lamp post

M IS ALSO FOR: Map, monkey, monocle, monster, moustache, museum

N IS ALSO FOR: National Gallery, necklace, newspaper, newsstand

O IS ALSO FOR: Octopus, onion, ostrich

P IS ALSO FOR: Pear, penguin, people, phone box, pigeon, pizza restaurant, post box, poster

Q IS ALSO FOR: Queue, quiche, "quiet please" sign, quilt

R IS ALSO FOR: Rain, reading glasses, red wine, roast beef, roast potatoes, rose, royals

S IS ALSO FOR: Sailor, screen, sky, sportsmen, sprinters, stands, sun

T IS ALSO FOR: Taxi, Thames, tiger, Tower of London, traffic, tugboat

U IS ALSO FOR: Ukulele, umbrella, uniforms, Union Jack

V IS ALSO FOR: Van, video camera

W IS ALSO FOR: Wasp, wellies, whites, worm

X IS ALSO FOR: X marks the spot, x-ray, xylophone

Y IS ALSO FOR: Yawn, yellow, yoga, yoghurt, yo-yo

Z IS ALSO FOR: Zebra, zookeeper

LONDON LANDMARKS
FEATURED IN THIS BOOK

Big Ben

The British Museum

Buckingham Palace

Downing Street

The Gherkin

The Houses of
Parliament

Hyde Park

Kew Gardens

King's Cross Station

Leicester Square

The London Aquarium

The London Eye

London Zoo

The National Gallery

Nelson's Column

The Olympic Park

Oxford Circus

Piccadilly Circus

Regent's Park

St Paul's Cathedral

The Serpentine

Shakespeare's Globe

The Statue of Eros

The Thames

Tower Bridge

The Tower of London

Trafalgar Square

Westminster Bridge

Wimbledon

OTHER LANDMARKS
FOR YOU TO VISIT

The Albert Memorial

Apsley House

The Bank of England

The Barbican

Battersea Power
Station

The British Library

Broadcasting House

Carnaby Street

Charing Cross

City Hall

Cleopatra's Needle

Covent Garden

Cutty Sark

Fortnum & Mason

Foyles

Green Park

Hamleys

Hampstead Heath

Hampton Court

Harrods

HMS Belfast

Highgate Cemetery

Horse Guards Parade

Imperial War Museum

Kensington Palace

Liberty

Little Venice

Lloyd's of London

The London Dungeon

The London Transport
Museum

Lord's Cricket Ground

Madame Tussauds

The Mall	The Royal Albert Hall
Mansion House	The Royal Observatory
Marble Arch	The Royal Opera House
The Millennium Bridge	The Science Museum
The Monument	Selfridges
The Museum of London	Smithfield Market
The National Maritime Museum	Spitalfields Market
The National Portrait Gallery	South Bank
The National Theatre	The Southbank Centre
The Natural History Museum	Southwark Cathedral
The O2	Speaker's Corner
The Old Bailey	St James's Palace
The Oxo Tower	St James's Park
Paddington Station	Tate Britain
Peter Pan in Kensington Gardens	Tate Modern
Portobello Market	Theatreland
The Ritz Hotel	Twickenham
	The V & A
	Wembley Stadium
	Westminster Abbey